THE QUITTERS

THE QUITTERS

CARLO MATOS

TORTOISE BOOKS
CHICAGO, IL

Once you quit, nothing is ever the same again. The euphoria is addictive; you develop an appetite for volition; you lose a certain innocence.

— Evan Harris, *The Quit*

Dead Man's Chest

"On one wall, a mirror. You've bled here, you've set others to bleed. We replace justice with a conflagration."

— Sara Tracey, "Tim (the Fighter)"

I.

Our gym, like all the others, is a single-masted sloop, manned to the timbers by an ardent crew of saw-toothed corsairs, each with their own colorful pirate pseudonym. There's "The Professor," for example, so called not because he's a fighter with a laconic and exacting style, but rather a writing teacher who never ceases complaining about all the grading he has to do after practice. There's also "Brain" (orthonym: Brian), a former high school wrestler who wonders unabashedly why so many jiu-jitsu practitioners speak "Brazilian." And then there's "The Face"—a Mexican-American Adonis, shredded and perfect despite subsisting entirely on McDonald's and Burger King—another stud wrestler we put on all our posters and promotional materials. (Of course, he earned the moniker by spending more time flexing in the mirror than training, which ended up garnering him a second nickname: "One-Round Rudy.")

It is beyond foolhardy to resist a name; they are powerful when unbidden, and unstoppable when unwanted. It follows a distinctly high school kind of logic. (If some dipshit upperclassman thinks you look like the patriarch of the Addams Family and decides one day that you are "Gomez," you know full well to accept it with a smile, and maybe even embrace it, putting it on your team hat and embroidering it on your varsity jacket because rejection would put you at risk of a baser alternative.) So if you're christened "The Robot" because you are equal parts long limbs and stiff joints, don't fight it, because then it mutates into "Frankenstein" and devolves finally to "Bender"—the hard drinking, foul-mouthed automaton from *Futurama*. If you're "Nosebleed," then be the best "Nosebleed" you know how—or "Wolfie," or "Sleepy," or "Danzo," "Weasel," "Johnny 5," "Too Tan," "Keith Sweat," "Sunshine," or "Punch-Your-Mother." Wear it until it becomes you because in fighting there is likely someone who shares that name and is at the ready to sink one more pretender. One day, you're "Ice Man"—cold, remote, untouchable—and the next, you're "Ice Man"—fragile, cracking under the slightest pressure. Best to batten down the hatches and fight—keep delaying the day your colors will burn, or worse, sink to the Challenger Deep, splintered by a newer, faster man o' war.

II.

As much as I admire Ptolemy's nested spheres and his epicycles (as byzantine and elegant as a boxer's angles and half-turns), and as much as I love Galileo going toe-to-toe with a pope, the man I remember most from middle school science class is Tycho Brahe—the scientist so badass he lost most of his nose in a duel and simply slapped on another one of silver and gold and went about his day.

Fighters know about noses; we can spot our own by the obtuse angles at which they often set. A well-placed strike can make blood shoot out in an ion stream or make your eyes water and leave you seeing stars; it all depends on how you're hit. My nose, for example, has been broken three times by uppercuts—twice during actual fights. The first time I broke it, I stopped snoring. The second time, my nose was straightened statue-perfect. The third time it set at a rakish angle, which I try to wear with a bravado and dignity worthy of Tycho himself. My teammate, Rudy, on the other hand, got his nose broken from a straight punch, which caused his nose to bridge and crest like the rim of a lunar crater. (Not even this impact could mar "The Face's" celestial good looks.) And then there's "Nosebleed," whose nose bleeds every practice even though no one has touched it—some unkind trick of physiognomy. Broken noses blaze brightly, to be sure; audiences hush to them, or are brought to anxious anticlimax by a contest that is most likely far from over. It is true the nose can turn almost any conversation to fighting, but it is the least of a fighter's worries. It is much worse to burst a hand, or rip a ligament in a knee, or throw out your back. The worst part of a broken nose is often the perfect bloom it leaves on a rose-white *gi*.

III.

The first person to get cauliflower ears was Tony, who we called "Too Tan" for his proclivity for hitting the tanning bed a little too hard before fight night.

We all knew it would have to happen sooner or later, but secretly, none of us were sure we were ready. Once the ears come in, that's it, you've crossed a line (a body suddenly and unexpectedly maturing), and there's no turning back—even if the blood is drained. There is no sound to match the pop an ear—a red seaweed pod—makes when it is punctured by the head coach's syringe, which is vastly preferable to what I did my first time, standing nude in front of the bathroom mirror with a sewing needle. As soft as ears look, they are tougher than a cowboy's face, and I am one of the lucky ones who, by sheer accident, didn't muscle the needle through my ear and into the side of my head—a common-enough experience, it turns out.

Then again, there are well-worn stories about what the ears can do for you in Brazil—jiu-jitsu capital of the world. People let you cut in line, and women throw themselves at you, or so I've heard. These may just be myths, I don't know, but we're happy enough to pass them down to the next generation.

The ancient Greeks knew all about it, of course. The *Terme Boxer*, a bronze statue circa 330 BCE, has both a broken nose and cauliflower ears. These features are badges of experience stamped small on the body itself, and even in America—the country of the plastic mask and perfect teeth—they can bond you to a complete stranger.

For example, one day a cop pulled Tony over on his motorcycle—a machine he had "accidentally" forgotten to register. The cop sat him down on the curb like a little boy: "You're done," he said, and walked to his cruiser. But as he was about to hand Tony the ticket, he paused: "Wrestling or jiu-jitsu?"

At first Tony had no idea what he was talking about, but he quickly realized he meant the ears. This was a delicate moment. Wrestlers and jiu-jitsu players are two grappling families historically antagonistic to each other. "Jiu-jitsu?"

The cop nodded and then did something we only find in our impossible fantasies as we sit in dead traffic—he ripped up the ticket. He left, honoring the hours implied

by an ear roughed up on the fresh coral, the ocean floor
of the brackish gym mats.

IV.

After a while, you won't even notice the notches in your shins. And so what if your hands hurt when it rains? And who cares if your left heel never stops aching? (The Greeks knew what they were about when they gave one of their invincible demigods a suspect heel: Achilles ankle-dangled over the River Styx by his mother, Thetis. They almost took Michael Jackson's children away when he pulled that same stunt from the balcony of his hotel— or was Michael's weak spot his hair, catching fire like Achilles' arteries when Paris made that one in a million shot with an arrow tipped in Hydra blood?) You've broken your nose so many times you don't even go to the doctor anymore, because she'll just give you the "What the fuck?" look, but—of course—MJ probably got the same treatment until he took that fat wad of cash out of his radiant glove. (Did you think it was just for selling records? Who would think to look for his stash there— his hand already in the glove?) The truth is sometimes we hide much in our hands: our heads in trouble, our faces in shame, our chins when punches fly free. A hand in a glove can do what the naked hand won't. It can clutch cold without freezing, cure without weakening, and, yes, strike without breaking.

V.

The technique for throwing knees in quick succession is quite similar to the Running Man—the ubiquitous late-80s kinetic dance craze popularized by crossover rappers like MC Hammer. On second thought, it's exactly the same. In the basement of my vavó's house, my double-first cousin Keith and I would create dance routines whose foundation and major content was the Running Man; we'd get down to the hip New Jack Swing of Bobbie Brown's "Every Little Step," or Neneh Cherry's sassy "Buffalo Stance," or even Stevie B's sweaty "Spring Love." We'd put those moves on display at weddings, which we attended wearing black turtlenecks (so as to better set-off the gold chains) layered beneath our matching V-neck sweaters, which cleverly rhymed with our gold-tipped dress shoes and pegged knockoff Z Cavarichi parachute pants. Who knew it would come in handy later in life? If only I could find the practical applications hidden in the Hully Gully or the Electric Slide—find all the missing steps to bridge the dance floor and the cage door.

VI.

There's that roguish streak in her hair—an awesome color a boy like him can't even name; it flashes wild like the way she hits his arms: recklessly, as if hoping they'd just fall off. (Hers or his, it doesn't quite matter.) He knows more about her knuckles than he does about her mother, or father, or whom she kissed first in some car out back somewhere. And that's how it is the moment before a punch lands, when it seems like the best idea— and maybe it is.

Most people give in before getting past her hip, vintage clothes and through to her perfectly executed bum. (One can't use a word any sharper than that for the way she looks in a dress. His ex-wife, on the other hand, has no bum but an ass, perfectly toned from hours at the vanguard of the roller derby track.) On Tuesdays, after beating the crap out of each other at kickboxing class, they go home—sometimes bloodied and bruised, always sore—and he skates that curve up her lower back, gripped like Brad and Angie in *Mr. & Mrs. Smith* after they shot the house full of holes and woke up the neighbors. And then they laze about exhausted, replaying the punches they took, the kicks they threw, who they wanted to take down, and who they wanted to take home. It was no surprise they were sometimes one and the same.

VII.

Every gym has an enforcer. It's not an official position; it's not a sought-after promotion or reward for dedication on the mats, but it seems to be as inevitable as ringworm, nonetheless. Someone just knows it's their job, and everyone else just tacitly accepts it. And it's never the person you think it is. It's not the huge guy with all the belts. It's not the gym star everyone thinks is going all the way. It's usually not a coach. It might be the old guy—a relative term at a fight gym, to be sure. It might be the woman who arrives at the gym covered in chalk dust with a backpack full of exams to grade. It could be the 120-pound five-foot-three guy we can never find an opponent for. It could be the pretty girl who looks like she got lost on her way to yoga or cardio kickboxing class. If your gym is run properly, you will not need the enforcer very often, but when the need arises, you will be glad you have one.

There are only a few instances in which the use of the enforcer is justified, and only when everything else has failed. In short, the enforcer is a last resort. Instance 1:

The talker. The talker seems utterly unaware of how disrespectful and distracting it is to talk at the same time the instructor is trying to teach technique. Not only do they talk during the explanations, they also talk during the drills. Instead of practicing, they are yammering away, thereby hampering their own progress and the progress of their partner. 2. The student teacher. This is the student who thinks they know better than the instructor. They will spend all class "correcting" their partner, often contradicting the instructor's advice. Most of the time, this person eventually stops coming, but when they don't, when they refuse to listen to the instructor who by now has pulled them aside a number of times to tell them to stop, it's time to let the enforcer do their work. And 3. The challenger. The challenger is the most insidious. This person thinks he—it's always a he—is the alpha in the room. He has a million war stories about his "street fights." He sometimes openly challenges the coaching staff and spars too hard with his partners, especially new people. He thinks it's his duty to show them something about being tough—like that one dad in the neighborhood who thinks kids today are too soft or have it too easy. That's when the enforcer innocently taps him for a sparring session and after a round or two (at most) politely accepts the new gloves the challenger leaves behind as trophies, trophies that will go into the box behind the boiler to be used by someone more deserving.

VIII.

MMA often disproves that macho line about acting one's size—certainly an even more dubious measure of wisdom than acting one's age. Technique can make a child of a hulking giant, reducing his once-terrifying bulk into a sweet deliquescence, swaddling him down into lullaby and sleep. For that brief moment in the cage or on the mats, the universe is brought back into proportion; one remembers that absolute sense of right and wrong one had at six, when the bad guys always lost, no matter their speed or strength or hideous malice. Of course, one must not fall for the lie that size doesn't matter, because it definitely CAN matter. You don't want to find out too late that a two hundred-pound brick-fisted opponent might as well be two hundred pounds of brick.

IX.

A fight isn't real until your name appears on the white board in simple dry-erase marker: dry-erase because the fight will most likely be rescheduled many times before the final date is set, and it's never as final as you'd like it to be anyway since most fighters can tell you a story about an opponent disappearing after weigh-ins the night before, or worse, vanishing the day of the fight, never to be seen again.

For now, the board simply reads "Rob Sucks," with three arrows pointing for added emphasis, but you know one day soon you will walk into the gym and reflexively glance at the board and there will be your name—your name and a date—nothing more. Nothing more is needed: a name, a date, a fact. You don't know why your throat catches—you knew it would be there. In fact, you have been waiting anxiously for this since you agreed to the fight a couple of weeks ago, ever since your coach approached you with the specifics, which in the amateur ranks never amounts to much. If you're able to learn the name of a potential opponent and find a fight or two on YouTube, you are lucky, but then again that name can change, and it might not really matter. Most of the time, the opponent—whomever it ultimately ends up being— is nothing more than a man to meet on the mat, someone who's spent their own weeks marked in black or red or green on a dry-erase board.

X.

The most important part of the fight is the ride over. Long before the walk-in music and the constant trips to the bathroom is the ride, in a down-and-out and duct-taped Ford Explorer on its last legs, but tempered like a kickboxer's shins. No menacing opponent's face, no worst-case scenario looms larger than your coach's voice as he becomes, for now, your dad—regardless of whether the real one was never there, or man enough to do his job without complaint or promise of return. The talk never varies and you are surprised to find adventure is not really the color of blood, nor is it the dark of the sea or the lure of distant lands, but a series of sweet platitudes long since memorized and unremarkable in every way, as unremarkable as the back seat of that bruised-blue Explorer where your problems are always serious, always solvable, but never small.

XI.

The real test of a fighter's resolve happens backstage while waiting his turn. Some prefer to fight right away; others need the time to relax and focus. Usually I am openly and unabashedly and almost dramatically nervous—so nervous my parents would call it "nerves," a not-so-subtle euphemism for emotional instability—so the longer the night goes on, the worse off I am. It is tedious to have to interrupt hand wrapping, pad hitting, and teammate bolstering to make frequent trips to the toilet, especially while wearing MMA shorts, which have vertical and lateral Velcro straps, plus laces, and then a cup beneath them to deal with. And there is often a long line of other dudes trying to look calm and avoid the nervous talking that sometimes overcomes new fighters. Every fight was like this—except the first one. For that fight, I wasn't nervous at all. I was bored, ready to be done, unconcerned, like I was in line at the grocery store. It wasn't confidence, I don't think. If you'd asked me how I was feeling, I would have probably shrugged. I could hear my coach's instructions, and I nodded at the correct moments, not really following along, but not confused either. The desired outcome was clear, even if the steps were lost on me. Maybe I was too old to be embarking on a fighting career, but I knew what it was like to perform under pressure. I had pitched as a kid, always getting picked for the second-to-worst baseball team—teams so bad that if the ball left the infield, it was at least a triple and probably an in-the-park homer—and yet I did manage to win a game or two. In high school, I was a tennis player better known for my screaming tantrums and racquet throwing than for my skills on the court. I wasn't the kid who ripped his team shirt Hulkamania-style when he lost a match, but I was close enough. I knew how to perform under pressure and I knew how to crack under it too, but here I was waiting in line, cashing a check or making a money order for the groceries like my parents used to do every Friday night.

XII.

I don't remember walking out to the cage. I don't remember what song was playing. I don't remember the cage door locking. I remember the bell ringing and then getting hit with a wild right. It was a really lousy punch, yet he caught me on the temple and then the mat began to tip towards my ear. And for some reason, instead of defending myself, I'm thinking about the standardized test I took in second grade where I misread the word "sweater" as "sweeter." The whole time I'm reading about this kid's new *sweeter* that he ultimately leaves at the park or something, and I have no clue what is going on. I don't even know what the test is for. I'm just following along, filling in little holes, and thinking about the seesaw balancing record my best friend and I are going to break at recess. It's at this point that I became vaguely aware of my opponent trying to choke me. A couple of weeks after the test, my teacher tells me I should go to this special room where Craig and I would prepare presentations on space shuttles, write papers about California condors, and perform puppet shows like the *Three Billy Goats*

Gruff for the kindergarten and first-grade students. And I could read all the books I wanted instead of copying sentences off the board. The choke got tighter. If he blew out his arms on this choke attempt, he'd be left with empty *sweeter* sleeves, waving to no effect like those one-legged air dancers car dealerships were so fond of. The choke, however, was dangerously tight now. Some part of me was aware of being in trouble; I got the gist, but by the time I made the move to get out, it was too late. And then I woke up.

XIII.

He walked in, but not out.

I was calling the fights that night because I had broken my right hand a couple of weeks earlier getting ready for the finals of the 2011 Team Challenge. Our team went up 2-1 quickly. "The Mechanic" tuned up his overmatched opponent in one round. "Too-Tan" was in a dogfight until he caught his opponent's chin with a knee that blacked him out in round 2. "No Mercy," sadly, pled for some after running out of gas in a fight he was dominating. All we needed to do was win the next fight. If this had been a movie, they would have won match four, and the last one would have come down to an insane Rock 'Em Sock 'Em Robots finish with the good guys snatching victory in the final seconds. But that is not how it went.

This would have been my fight if I had not hurt myself punching "The Face" in the face a few weeks back. It was clear right away that Rudy's wrestling was too much for this kid. Barely a minute into round 1, Rudy caught his back in a standing rear naked choke, and that was it. (If

Rudy catches you in the first round, he's a finisher—the other reason we called him "One Round Rudy.") Although a dominant position, having to ride piggyback requires stamina—something Rudy never had a lot of.

But the other kid didn't know that. Whether it was the pressure of the moment, the earnest desire to keep his team in the tournament, or just a lack of technical understanding—whatever the reason—it would be both his last day as a competitor, and mine. When Rudy's opponent bent over, as if bowing to the audience (as if making a grand exit), trying to illegally spike Rudy on his head, he forgot to take into account that Rudy's center of gravity and his own were not in line. When he passed the midway point of his bend, gravity took over and then there was no way to stop the meteoring to the canvas. He landed right in front of my commentary position, his head twisted in an acute angle under Rudy's weight. He didn't get up—not right away, not after the paramedics came in, not ever.

XIV.

Behind the cage is a box of broken-down abandoned junk gear we don't think too much about: an odd number of mismatched shin guards, gloves with dead Velcro, headgear barnacled and duct taped, a cup no one will touch (never mind claim), all in a box by the boiler. It's no one's idea of a treasure chest, to be sure, until the day you catch a glimpse of a glove you once loved, or a shin guard you almost didn't buy because you weren't sure you had earned it yet, one you'd seen on the borrowed fist or leg of some beginner, their face flush and bedazzled. They're holding their breaths and gasping, flinching from punches and yet running headlong into them, waiting desperately for the buzzer and hoping to God it'll never sound.

And you know—because you did it too—how those first nights will go. The night she punches her husband's sleeping back because she might be done, but her body isn't. Weeks, now months, waiting for that muscle memory stuff—just a clever way of forcing one more combination on the bag, one more run up the steps, one more teeth-clattering judo throw onto the mat—only to have her body fire off in sticky sleep. Or the shock the first time he snaps a triangle choke on someone and it catches his partner's face in the act of realizing there is no escape but to tap out or go under. Or the day she runs three miles without realizing it when before she couldn't break one, no matter how hard she tried. It doesn't last, of course.

Training is a grind of its own, but the longer you train, the more of you is in that box, worth the sweaty effort of digging. One day, when the fighting is done, all that will be left are the hands, the feet, the bones in negative relief in a box by the boiler.

The Quitters

"Every quit is a decision, but not every quit is a final decision."

— Evan Harris, *The Art of Quitting*

I.

Pain Eyre took her spot on the line, the panty a little crooked on her hockey helmet. She was a smallish girl but she wasn't very quick or agile and she only had a couple years on skates. Everyone held their breaths, crouched, and got ready to hit. She was a new jammer, and they were by far the most fun to watch.

II.

Jamming in roller derby is where the rubber meets the road. (Or in this case, the sport court.) Experienced jammers have learned how to test a jam, how to determine the proper energy output required to penetrate the opposing defense. They know from long hours on their quad skates which of the slower defensive members they might be able to scoot by, which of the hulking giants they might lure into a trap—feint one way and then, the moment their weight gives itself over to that side, snap back the other way. The best jammers develop an almost uncanny ability to sense an opening just before it happens, like a duelist hearing the click on the big clock before high noon. But they also know when they've been ensnared; they don't waste all their energy trying to release a clamp. (A defensive strategy by which two or three girls wall a jammer in, blocking escape and repelling her teammates as they batter away from the outside hoping to force an opening.) An experienced jammer will continue to probe for weaknesses, but if she's caught she'll know to save her energy. New jammers, on the other hand, are all enthusiasm, all top speed and full steam ahead. They imagine scoring countless points as the other jammer remains helplessly trapped at the back of the pack.

The reality, of course, is much more sobering. First they find fear—a sudden unreasonable desire to pass the starred panty (which marks them as it did Cain, even though their invulnerability is a dare, not a warning) to anyone nearby, even as they coolly slip it on over their glassy phallic helmets. Then the whistle and the immediate and suffocating feeling of running out of room as a cliff's edge of finely-tuned asses looms into view. If they are lucky or skilled enough to get through the first pass, they quickly realize as they skate the lonely ellipse back towards the pack that they must do it again and again, must inevitably fall headlong against a shore of hips as eternal as any in the long history of the sea.

III.

The whistle blew and Pain Eyre ran right into the defense, as did the other jammer, Sylvia Wrath. For a little while it looked like she was holding her own, and then Sylvia Wrath snuck by the inside line and right through the pack.

Pain was starting to panic. She could see Wrath out of the corner of her eye as she made her orbit and headed back towards the pack to start a scoring run. An experienced jammer would have known to relax and keep probing for a way through, or keep pushing her captors forward until they broke the pack formation, but Pain couldn't move these women far enough. They were just too good. Wrath went spread eagle and cut through like a cleaver and scored five easy points as Pain was spin cycled by the defense.

IV.

There are times the jammers don't make it through at all. They get clamped and spend the rest of the jam pressed like wine grapes, skins and all. And it must seem as though the opposing jammer is making short work of the defense, scoring untold points while they're stuck clumsily juking against helmeted monsters with clever pseudonyms like Jillenium Falcon or Neverending Tori. And, of course, the audience is always uniquely helpful, yelling advice like, "Get through" or "Push harder" or "Go around," as if it were somehow revelatory, as if it was a lack of understanding rather than the material reality of several hundred pounds of wheeled muscle blocking the open track. This is the time to watch the jammer most closely. This is where the quit will happen if it's going to happen. Some of the new girls, even as they sag from exhaustion, will continue to fight until the two minutes are up or the opposing jammer calls off the jam. Old man in the sea be damned; these girls come up for air among the sharks only to do it all over again two or three jams later. There is no quit in these girls. Even when common sense tells them to save their energy, they can't do it, can't convince themselves to hang back. And when they don't make it through, their stubbornness short-circuits their logic processing centers, refusing the building of crucial synapses, interfering with their ability to learn the lesson. The next jam will likely be the same, and the next one. As either Benjamin Franklin or Albert Einstein never famously said, "The definition of insanity is doing the same thing over and over and expecting it to come out different," but in this case it might be better than the alternative because those who learn the lesson of their first jams too easily tend to quit before they can develop the attitude of the raised fist. You can see it in their faces. When you're a part of the pack, personal failing can be hidden in the confusion of the mêlée—at least from the audience—but when you're the jammer, all is revealed, even to the least discerning eye. To some, being revealed in this way is worse than any hit or fall.

V.

It wasn't looking good, but then it happened. As Wrath was coming around for a second scoring pass, she got boxed for a penalty, which meant for the next minute Pain was free to score without having to worry about the other jammer. (This is called a power jam.) But first things first, she needed to get through this pack. With the help of the offense, she was finally able to break through and was slowly and exhaustedly approaching the pack— the beast of many backs. She knew she didn't have much time before Wrath was out of the box and X-winging it towards her six. She seemed determined not to be trapped. If she could escape once, she could do it again. (Simple logic works well under pressure. Simplify the situation; simplify your purpose. Give yourself one thing to do. That is what her coaches told her in practice.)

She began to pick up speed in order to use her size like a bowling ball. If she could knock down at least one girl, it would be that much easier to get those five points back. She came barreling in at top speed, got low, and took aim at the shortest blocker, who, unfortunately, saw her coming and jacked her shoulder right into Pain Eyre's solar plexus—a totally legal move called a can opener. The word "timber" flashed on the inside of her eyelids and she began to fall backwards.

VI.

Derby girls are taught to fall forward for a reason. Falling forward allows the skater to make use of her kneepads and wrist guards, which protects her from breaking her tailbone or hitting the back of her head against the floor. Derby is about skating, yes, but it is also about falling.

When you are fresh meat, you spend more time learning how to fall than learning crossovers or hockey stops. It is a game where progress can be measured in the number of falls you make. First you are taught to fall, then you are taught to stand back up. Talented skaters fall to a knee like they were born to it, like that dream where you just barely skim along the ground—not flying exactly but not touching the earth either.

VII.

Right before it happened, she had a premonition something was coming, like when you pull up to a double set of stoplights that serve no purpose: no intersection, no traffic, just a little half-street, an alley, a Starbucks.

It was like the first time she gave herself over to a crossover, really leaned into the centripetal force and her skate didn't catch as she sliced by the offending shoulder determined to push her outside the line, flaring like a coronal mass ejection on its way to the blue, blue earth, nearly as blue as her starred helmet panty. Or the time, and for no offense she could glean, when physics gave her the hip and sent her scorching towards some zealous fans in the suicide seats—faces painted topsy-turvy in the way of all zealots.

Like all zealots, she was built to bleed, made to test the iron in her will against the teeth of the track.

VIII.

From the stands, it didn't look like much. People fall in derby all the time. But when she didn't get up right away, everyone knew she was hurt. (Most nights there will be a skater or two shot off the track like a comet whipping around its perihelion, but those often turn out not to be the most devastating.) The skaters took a knee and silence descended on the track and in the audience. Even the jeerleaders knew this was not the time to taunt their opponents. Pain was down. When she fell, her leg had twisted beneath her, causing it to break just above the shoe line of the skate, a horrible spiral tib/fib fracture. She had months on crutches to look forward to.

Though we are told otherwise, there is also a price to pay when we don't know when to quit.

The Bull's Eye

"This bow will break the heart and spirit of many a man here"
— Homer, The Odyssey

I.

When you carry a bow, everyone wants to sit next to you, especially on a train. There's something in the shape of a recurve that makes people riding a bus imagine immeasurable steppes on horseback and the smell of wool and sheep's milk—their brown paper bags full to the brim with a rare *airag*. No one even cracks wise about Robin Hood, since his kind hasn't been seen in these woods for far too long. It's nothing to joke about anyway. People feel ready when you're near for whatever comes next. For although they might not be prepared, you, of course, would sling an arrow or light a fire, or drag them to water and out of the night because even bats don't scare you. A man with a gun is to be feared; a gun is undiscerning. But a man with a bow has gone out and come back, tested his aim and the tension of a string.

II.

I knew it the moment they began backing away—although I should have realized much sooner. It wasn't my fault. My right eye had been twitching for nearly a week solid.

The place was packed on a Thursday afternoon, and I was smashed right up against the wall, right next to a guy who was shooting a procession of arrows blind, each penetrating the butcher paper masking his target and hitting all his marks. My first half-dozen shots were bank shots, Wild West at its best had they hit the correct target. Try looking like you deserve that gear you bought while waiting in line to fetch your arrows from your neighbor's target. Archers don't ride tandem for good reason. Then I stuck one in an impossible corner—the fletching facing 45 degrees across the line of fire. My poor arrow tips were taking the brunt of the action, and I just kept flinging them and pushing chance to its limits until it was about to break into luck—what kind was up for grabs.

It wasn't until I was in bed later that night that I realized I batted righty the entire session. Although I am right handed, I shoot with the other hand. I learned lefty— something to do with a dominant eye. I shot against logic for hours and wasn't torn to shreds. This was how it was when I was a child, no way to argue a case, any case, and yet unable to adapt or adjust, only survive. The only recourse was omission: a paltry weapon, easily deflected by those who needed only to get the last word, who had selective hearing, who could take anything except blame, whose asses never seemed to sweat in the heat, who didn't mind the sun digging into their eyes or the feel of wool on their skins. No noise was too loud, not even the string twanging against the corners of their mouths. Then, as now, the safest place to be was right in front of the target, staring the bull's eye down until it charged.

In the Hippo's Mouth

"Time passes very slowly when you're in a hippo's mouth"
— Paul Templer

I.

Whenever I dream about my father, I end up thinking of André—as in André the Giant. I blame *The Princess Bride*. As Peter Falk tells his sick grandson, it truly has everything: "Fencing, fighting, torture, revenge, giants, monsters, chases, escapes, true love, miracles"—not to mention a Spanish sword master, a fierce princess, a dread pirate, and, of course, gentle Fezzik, played by the one and only André Roussimouff.

André and my father, it turns out, had a lot more in common than I was aware of in 1987. Before turning to wrestling, André had been a humble worker, a factory man assembling engines for hay balers, though none to lay siege to those who never tired of reminding him of the obvious; my father, too, worked anonymously, pressing suits he would never wear to armor the bodies of those who wouldn't look to spit on him. But I did not know any of this then. There was only Fezzik, the hippopotamic landmass from Greenland with a great gift for rhyme.

As a young man in the Azores, my father also built walls by hand by day—fitting stones like Antaeus mortaring skulls to roof the temple he was building to his father, Poseidon—and performed plays by night in the village with his seven siblings. As for André, he did not act before coming to America, but in a way the stage came to him; he was so tall he couldn't take the bus to school, so he had to be driven in a truck by his neighbor—the playwright, Samuel Beckett.

My father and Fezzik both made their way to the United States in the end; there, André finally found a place vast enough for him to stand up straight, for once not having to crouch or crunch or bend, while my father—not a big man to begin with—continued to collapse in on himself, shoulders pointing in like the dipoles of a horseshoe magnet.

II.

They do in fact look alike, despite the nearly 400-pound differential. They even sound alike, speaking a sweet-bottomed English, fat and slow-tongued like a sag of hippos nosing at the surface of the Zambezi River.

My father is not dead, at least not in the material sense, but I know that André is, and the part of me that misses him is the same part of me that wanted Hulk Hogan to scoop slam the Giant in WrestleMania III—until he actually did. It is the same part of me that laments the failure of an old Louisiana congressman's fabled plan to seed the bayou with pods of hippopotami—a scheme which fell apart because of a forgotten rivalry, something André didn't know too much about, since his feuds have grown into legend. When the formerly undefeated 520-pound giant finally bloated down to the canvas (tearing Hogan's latissimus dorsi in real life despite losing the fake match), he was my father pinned to the couch waiting for another week to start, and Hogan was like a man half-swallowed by a hippo and then spit out—a would-be

Jonah leaving behind one of his arms in the river that made his living.

Portuguese Paradise

"He then thought of freezing a jump. As though it were possible to suspend the force of gravity, if only for an hour (he did not ask for any more than that)"

—Gonçalo M. Tavares, *The Neighborhood*

I.

I didn't even know there were any Portuguese in California until I moved there. I thought they only lived in the Northeast and select parts of Canada—all the places I had played *festas* in until I was a junior in high school. (My feet ache at the memory of all those polyester dirges on streets covered in flower petals like byzantine tiles.) And yet, the whole year I lived in the Central Valley, I never actually met a single Portuguese, never uttered a single word in the language that had languished for so many years since I'd left home. Even the so-called Portuguese restaurant in Modesto wasn't really Portuguese. It was some kind of generic European fare, hardly Portuguese at all. Something was clearly different about our *primos* on the West Coast, or maybe I was looking in the wrong place.

II.

In Fall River, we were out in the open. Go to Little Portugal, or what the city officially designated the "Cultural District" (bounded by the Three Gates, the *igreja de Santo Cristo*, and the Braga Bridge—the longest bridge in the United States because it goes from Fall River to Portugal, or so the old joke goes) and you can hear us from tenement windows, yelling loud and fast. (It's even too much for most New Englanders, who are usually pretty speedy talkers themselves, who live to interrupt, and who are not afraid to use *fortissimo* to make even the most minor point. We always sound like we're arguing, and sometimes we are.) The bakeries, the church bells, the old men in fedoras and the widows in black— powerful women even the gangbangers left alone; we were out in the open. But there seemed to be none of that in the valley. Nothing in Merced or Modesto, nothing in San Francisco, Oakland or Fresno.

Or maybe I didn't go looking. I didn't think about this until I was long gone and living in the Midwest, where no *padrões* asterisked the history books with pictures of long ships with those blood-red crosses on white sails.

III.

On the West Coast, there is also Pismo Beach—
"Portuguese Paradise," I heard it called—a beach
community where Portuguese supposedly have summer
homes. Of course, I pictured the East Coast again; I
imagined Cape Cod, *Mystic Pizza*, rich Anglos in
cottages, working Portuguese and clambakes, quahogs
and periwinkles. (To be honest, most of the Portuguese I
knew weren't even fishermen anymore, but mill
workers.) But Pismo sounded like something altogether
different. My friend said his "rich" friends were
Portuguese.

Rich Portuguese? I had never met one. I had never
imagined such a thing. In my little piece of
Massachusetts, we worked; we made do; we stretched our
pennies; we kept ahead of the next closing mill. We dug
in our heels. We did our best and knew that it still wasn't
enough, that it was an admission of defeat. We made do;
we jumped on the hoods of cars and marked the muggy-
bug nights with our sweat.

IV.

It must've been the Super Mario craze that made us mad for jumping on the hoods of cars. We spent most nights one summer in a parking lot pressed between the band house stoop on Hope Street (where we earnestly practiced John Philip Sousa tunes in a dense harbor of smoke) and the church on Columbia Street. We practiced, kissed each other's sisters, smoked cigarettes stolen from the corner store, and had all-out fistfights to pass the time. And we hopped cars. Maybe those two mustachioed, blue-collar plumbers-turned-heroes—who looked so much like our fathers and uncles—were proof that we could win a princess or two, that being outsiders didn't automatically make us the bad guys. Or maybe we just liked raging from car to car since none of us could actually afford a Nintendo Entertainment System. (Or, for that matter, the superfluous robot in the television commercial that inexplicably dropped a little top.) Because sometimes we felt invincible as we soared from one car to another or grew double size to safely stomp on those who belonged.

V.

As for our West Coast *primos*, their dads were in the dairy industry; they were ranchers or farmed cow feed. But they had Pismo. (In Fall River, all they had was the "Cultural District." A far cry from paradise, to be sure.)

I didn't know it at the time, but I guess I really didn't want to go there. I didn't go searching for paradise because I didn't know how I'd face a Portuguese who had planted his flag firmly in the soil of an America that had never quite been so welcoming to those I knew, an America that didn't quite live up to Emma Lazarus's words carved in the sweat of so many immigrants.

Or maybe it wasn't that at all. Maybe I was afraid it wasn't true and that all of my cousins out west had found the land dug deep with stones, udders dry and the desert thankless and full of thorns.

The Others

"Won't you show me where it hurts / I'm not angry anymore"
—Blair's Carriage, "Lori's Curb"

I.

Our youths are secure in the darkness of the pre-internet age; we grew up in the faceless mystery of the 90s, a decade of extreme alienation.

It didn't feel good at the time to be so isolated from the normal course of things, but it was far superior to the tedious hyper-connectivity we have today. Before Facebook, before Twitter, before Tumblr, before Tinder, we spent a lot of time secretly wondering what others were really thinking. It gave us purpose, or something very much like it. We listened to music hoping to touch the part of people we couldn't reach with our hands. It gave us a reason to read books, maybe. It gave us a reason to look at paintings. There was even a purpose in going to church, though not the one our parents would have wanted. When you don't know what others are thinking, you can assume their thoughts are profound, nuanced, odd, interesting—or at the very least, more profound and interesting than your own. You can accept your own banality, because they must know things you don't, or do things you can't. The less someone said, the better, for you might be petty, lazy, and simple, but not everyone could be like you, right? There had to be others who were thinking things through. There had to be others who were courageous and forthright. There had to be someone who didn't quit. There had to be.

II.

His name was Scott. He was a solo act. Unlike the members of my band, he didn't look like a kid, although he was clearly still in high school. He had chin-length dirty-blond Alice-in-Chains hair, and a tattoo of a sun on the wrist of his fretting hand. (I wanted a tattoo so bad, but I was too young. It's hard to be cool and front a rock band when your parents won't even let you get an earring, never mind a tattoo.)

When he started to sing, I wanted to rush on stage and squeeze the life out of him. I wanted to pummel him to death. I wanted to abduct him. I wanted to sell all my worldly possessions, shave my head, and travel the land spreading his word. I wanted to start a war in his name. I wanted to write an epic poem about the mythical founding of his country—Scotland. Nothing else would do.

I knew it as soon as he played "Lemonade," and "Baseball," and "Tepid," songs few people would ever hear, each one as perfect as if it had always just been there. I had been waiting for these songs all my life. I had been hearing them in the background static as I fell asleep. They were simple tunes. There was nothing fancy about them, but they had everyone in the small audience in his power, not that he seemed to notice. I felt embarrassed to have just been on the stage. How could we compete with him? He was the first person I ever met that I knew was going to "make it" in that cheesy, American Dream, big movie, "I'm-going-to-California" kind of way. It was inevitable. Talent of this kind must get out or it must explode. Even an unjust universe must acknowledge talent like this and if not, then it wasn't worth a damn.

III.

His name was Scott, and he was also the lead singer of a band named Blair's Carriage. Scott with eyes closed. Scott with a cigarette jammed in the head of his guitar. Scott singing about a girl named Lori. After he finished his set, we went looking for him. We didn't know what we were going to say because we would have said anything. We didn't know what we were going to do because we would have done anything. When we finally spotted him, he was in a swing next to a pretty pixie of a girl who, it turns out, was the violin player in his band, though we didn't know that at the time. I knew she must be the eponymous Lori of "Lori's Curb." I wanted it to be Lori. I needed it to be Lori. I just knew she would be something. She would have to be too much or never mind. I knew he wouldn't be the kind of guy to date groupies like I would do years later when we finally got good enough. He wouldn't do that. He was bigger than that—better.

IV.

They swung slowly, moved with the rhythm of playground swings in a gentle wind.

Behind us the last band played on the rented truck bed, but we could no longer hear them. We stood in a line, staring unselfconsciously like children often do upon first meeting, unable to approach but unable to quit the scene. "You're in my bathtub," we heard her say—the weird childish jargon we used when swinging in perfect tandem—and Scott laughed so casually we all lost something, like we died standing upright, turned to salt by a power we did not understand—or much worse, could never understand.

The sun continued setting like it does. No one laughed. No one cried. No great bolt of lightning split a tree. No prayers were given and none received. No one had anything more to say. We walked away. We went home. We didn't know; life began.

Smells Like Teen Spirit

"Load up on guns, bring your friends / It's fun to lose and to pretend"

—Nirvana, "Smells Like Teen Spirit"

I.

I admit I don't understand people with school spirit. It seems to be a defining trait: there are people who have it and people who don't. Then again, this could be a false binary. Shibboleths sound good in theory, but this kind of thinking has its perils—forty and two thousand bodies in the River Jordan and all that.

For people with school spirit, the event—whether it's a sporting contest, a school rally, a political affair, or a religious gathering—is all about identity, about publicly supporting a side. In sporting events, for example, although winning is the ostensible endgame, it is largely a ruse—a self-imposed one to be sure, but a ruse nonetheless. People with school spirit will go bananas if they win, it's true, but they will go equally wild if they lose. The outcome of the game, as far as I can tell, is arbitrary.

When I was in college, my best friend Sean and I were making our way back to the dorms one night, not realizing that some important sporting event had just concluded. We found the dorms literally aflame. Students were actually heaving burning couches from lounges; broken glass misted along on drifts of smoke. Six thousand students lived in a complex of towers that were twenty-six stories high, so some of these couches were meteoring down and landing with devastating explosive force, sending flaming debris among the mob of drunken students: some crying, some yelling, some chanting, some crawling among the wreckage and moaning like mendicants. And then Sean and I noticed imposing, faceless shadows all around the dark perimeter, ready like Odin's hat for the slaughter; police on horseback had surrounded the dorms in order to contain the carnage to school grounds. We love to throw around the word "apocalypse" these days, but that scene remains the closest I've ever gotten to it—apocalypse as poor imitation of a Bosch painting, with all the figures clad in Abercrombie & Fitch or pajama pants: a fantasy worthy of one of those end-of-days cults who worship at the hooves of the pale rider. And yet, through some miracle (and in spite of youthful ignorance), death did not gallop in that night. I didn't want to calculate those odds. It's wise not to calculate the odds for miracles.

II.

We were largely unaware that we had a very good basketball team that year, since basketball was number three on our list of most tedious sports to watch, after football and golf. Still, it did help explain the presence of the five or six towering figures we were constantly running into in the bathroom—the great social equalizer of the campus community. The bathrooms were not meant to be coed, but the sheer amount of puke splattered in shower and toilet stall alike often forced us to share any shower that somehow survived the previous night's purge.

Finding such a shower was a challenge, like an early-morning scavenger hunt made tedious by constant repetition. The math was nonlinear and the equations got away from us very quickly. Sean and I had a weekly pool in which we tried to predict which shower stall on which floor would survive the weekend unmolested. I'd learned a ton about statistical analysis that semester, and about how difficult predictions are to make no matter how much data you have. Apparently, however, both women and men shared the same disgusting proclivity for marking their territory after a night of binge drinking two-dollar pitchers of cheap beer. We tried to be very blasé about it—we were very worldly, after all—but I admit to having a very clear memory of the first time I showered next to a person of the opposite sex, as if it were some kind of rite of passage. And maybe it was, like the painted faces, the chanting, and the returning home to get a good night's sleep and resume one's normal life.

This last part seemed key. Though there were times when school spirit turned ugly, went full-blown hooligan, the normative experience was not one of violence, even though it needed to carefully verge on the lips of violence. Sometimes, even though we are told otherwise by every beer commercial and Facebook meme, we must know when to quit. It must be proximal to mass violence but never cross the boundary.

It was a Christmas kind of dedication: one day of intensely fraught fellowship, and then back to the grind as if nothing much had happened. The next day, they went about their business looking askance and slightly confused by the wreckage that survived the night, memories of flames framed in darkness now fading under the light of the morning, the clock struck dumb from repeated blows.

Yankee Swap

The isle is full of noises,
Sounds, and sweet airs, that give delight and hurt not.
Sometimes a thousand twangling instruments
Will hum about mine ears; and sometime voices.
                    —William Shakespeare, *The Tempest*

A Yankee swap is a particularly nefarious thing. It's a game that pretends not to be a game, which always carries peril. What begins in good faith very quickly turns ugly, like when poor Carrot Top was scorched during those abortive reboots of the celebrity roasts on Comedy Central. It begins with laughter; oh, it always begins with laughter, which grows increasingly pinched and then slowly becomes hostile and embarrassing as people fight over the one gift brought by the person who refuses to follow the rules and actually brings something "nice." There is always one.

This seems to be an inviolable law of the universe, and it certainly held true for this particular event, although I am pretty sure had all the gifts been properly ridiculous, there would still have been fierce competition, as if the entire point of the exercise was to trigger the aggressive displays of greater primates for research purposes. (There are few things as anxiety-inducing to a working-class kid than the giving and receiving of gifts. When you don't have money, you teach yourself not to want or expect anything. It's automatic, like some adaptive trait being suddenly and violently activated by the correct environmental stimulus. No one wants to press their face to the proverbial candy-shop window over and over with no way to satisfy the craving. Fuck Tantalus. He was a fool.) I looked around the table and saw the aching faces stuck in primate play grins that had long since become tortured and painful. My grin was cutting across my face and into my eyes.

II.

I was not expecting the night's dinner (a joint English and Theater department affair to welcome a new faculty member) to be any different than the countless others that had preceded it. I was seated between the new professor—a seat of honor, I suppose, but not one I was happy to receive—and an incredibly tall and sharp-angled man who, judging by his ramrod-straight spine, I wasn't going to like. (In my experience, people with good posture are not to be trusted. I've always been Caliban by comparison, Richard Crookback, or maybe Quasimodo.) I even turned my chair slightly away from him in the hopes of dissuading casual conversation. He turned out to be her husband, though I couldn't for the life of me see those two together in any context except for a crime scene photo. Thankfully he took up with my friend, a fellow denizen of the Research Center whose southern charm made her a natural at these events. She once again spared me from awkward and stilted conversation, but I don't remember repaying her in any way that would make up for this service rendered. (I am not good at these things—not by design, not necessarily. Some of it is clearly due to a lack of real-world experience. As the son of immigrants, I had very little interaction with highly educated people. In fact, I had few experiences with any adults who were not directly related to me. The rest of it was clearly genetic. My family was a decidedly sour bunch, unable to muster much enthusiasm about things that weren't immediately relevant to them; our table manners were both more antique and baroque than our American peers, and yet somehow more off-putting. My parents think Americans don't know how to use a knife and a fork. To them, Americans look like little children trying to spear a hotdog piece with a shaky hand, or barbarians covered in animal fur stabbing hunks of freshly slaughtered meat with the same implement they used to kill the animal with in the first place.)

III.

"I'm Miranda," she said, but I didn't realize quickly enough she was talking to me. She had been in casual conversation with the man to her right, who was also one of my professors, and I didn't notice the moment they went silent. Though I recovered, I didn't do so in time, and she definitely noticed. I managed to stammer my name and offer her my hand—a stupid gesture when you're sitting at a dinner table. (I might as well have lowered my head and held out my palm to show submission, like chimps do.) She smiled anyway and took it and I felt, at least, that she was a generous person. There was no judgment in her eyes, nor any intrinsic need to mock me or to assert her dominance or rank.

Of course, the problem is that I don't really like nice people. Nice is so often a euphemism for weakness or dullness. It's not that I like cruel or rude people, because I don't. Her husband fit into both these categories and I wanted to punch him in the mouth from the moment I heard him speak, but nice people (though they often mean well) tend to have no other dimension, as if "niceness" is so much hard work (and I am sure that it actually is) that it's impossible to have any other interests or ambitions. That is, if they're sincere. There are many "nice" people who hide their hideous malice behind a well-rehearsed upturning of the lips—not really a smile at all but a grimace, a toothy rictus out of some nature show.

IV.

Somehow—and I'm convinced all great conversations start this way—somehow, we got onto a shared topic. Here it was *The Tempest*. The department was mounting a new production this semester that Miranda was dramaturging. It didn't arise from any of her previous questions about my work, or my lame replies, or my less-than-sincere aping of her questions. It came of its own volition, as if to save us from the sheer horror of the Yankee Swap.

The transition was lost. We were lost in transition. I don't remember what ideas we discussed. I don't remember the nuances of our disagreement, nor where our ideas came together and bloomed into pretty conclusions and secret acquiescence. What I do remember is how close our faces were to touching, and that I was nearly sitting on her lap. And our knees had been in direct contact for some time without me realizing. I didn't want to break the circuit. I could feel her breath on my eyelashes and in the stubble of my five-o'clock shadow. I suddenly became aware of the fact that I was sweating, visibly sweating—the kind of movie sweat that looks like fully-formed tears, and I couldn't stop it. I was dabbing at my forehead with a napkin like a Tennessee Williams character, like how I imagine Big Daddy when he confronts Brick about his drinking in *Cat on a Hot Tin Roof*. My knees were starting to ache from the awkward way we were sitting, and my back was stiff from leaning into the wind of her voice, but I wouldn't have changed position for anything, fearing I might remind her that this was not how one behaves at the dinner table. My mother would have been scandalized. Proximity wasn't the issue, nor the coveting of thy neighbor's wife, but the sin of ignoring one's hostly duties was. Turning your back on your guests is an ancient and serious crime. Of course, I'm not sure we were very aware that we were at the table anymore.

And it was perfectly innocent, from a certain perspective, anyway—as tends to be the case with innocence. We never left the topic of Shakespeare, never left the acceptable realm of academic discourse—that is, if one were only listening to the words, like a true sixteenth-century audience member would have. (As my professor was fond of telling us, "In the Renaissance, people went to *hear* a play.") But if you were watching our body language, if you were Jane Goodall in a baobab tree, for example, you'd be *seeing* quite a different show.

V.

I wanted her very, suddenly, badly. I wanted to throw her down on the table and make everyone watch us have nasty Shakespearean-themed sex, hoisting our own petards and unsexing her husband, accents and all. She was British, so hers, at least, would be authentic, which only made me want her more. Authenticity was so fucking hot.

But to be honest, I was afraid, too. Was I not just pressing my face against the department store window, even if in this case the mannequin had come to life and was touching her hand against the other side of the glass like in that silly 1980s movie with the Jefferson Starship soundtrack? Because clearly she wasn't going to take me on this table, Yankee Swap me for her husband, and clearly I wasn't going to be able to secret her away to my small desk upstairs while he was sitting next to me, at least not without him trying to figure out how to beat me to death without getting caught.

And, saddest of all, the likelihood that we would ever be able to recreate a moment like this one was rather remote. How many times can Shakespeare reasonably give birth to a great romance off the stage? (For I knew already it was a great romance.) The night ended much too quickly, and all I had to show for it was a sore jaw, aching knees, and a stiff neck.

VI.

Miranda went down hard. It happened so suddenly that for a second I thought she was dead. There was no attempt at recovery at all. She was midsentence and then she was down, like when the line goes dead in a horror movie, or the TVs blink out as alien ships descend on our favorite monuments. No one had noticed that a previous instructor had placed one of those tabletop podiums on the floor.

(These were common in many classrooms and most teachers found them annoying—relics of some misinformed person's idea of what a classroom should look like. Classroom: chalkboard. Check. Pointer. Check. Podium. Check. We have classroom. The only teachers who actually used podiums were those unlucky enough to land the large introductory classes, where lecture was the only possible mode of transmitting knowledge. When I was an undergraduate, a student had a sandwich delivered to our Astronomy 101 class and the teacher was so far away he had no idea. And it wasn't his fault; there were almost 300 students in that lecture hall and he would have needed binoculars to see what was going on or maybe a telescope. But in small classes, a podium is largely useless.)

The podium was located in such a way that when Miranda rounded the corner of her desk she flipped almost head over heels. I wanted to reach out to her. I wanted to help her to a chair, but instead I fell into a fantasy of catching her in my arms as she plummeted to the floor, which then triggered the fantasy I'd been having for weeks where I'd make my move on her late one night during rehearsals for *The Tempest*. (Performing is fun but rehearsal is where the real action is. Rehearsal is all lips and ears and the sanctioning of teeth against the granite of the script. Rehearsal is where only is only, where sudden becomes suddenly, where summer has horns and winter burrs. It is where backstage is lit and lilting like a slide trombone, like the pen-scrawled love letter you find in a junk drawer as an adult.) Once again, I was Caliban: disfigured, unloved, and cast about by greater powers.

VII.

I just sat there like a moron. I was afraid something would be revealed if I was too solicitous or concerned, so I did nothing until others sprang into action. I wondered how often people held back for fear of such revelations, and how many times that got others hurt. Miranda stood up, comically dusted herself off, and resumed class as if nothing much had happened; we were happy and relieved to play along. However, as the class neared its end, I noticed that she was cradling her left arm like a mother chimp with a new baby, and she went from pale to blanched. I could see sweat forming over her top lip, but she didn't lose a second of instruction time.

When we saw her the following week, she was sporting a cast. She had taught most of a class with a severely broken arm. I had an incredible desire to ask her if I could sign it, like we did in junior high school when we were all breaking bones, but not yet breaking hearts.

VIII.

She left not terribly long after arriving: a year, two years. I don't remember. Did I kiss her? No. Maybe I did. Let's say I did. No, let's say she kissed me and then I knew what innocence was and why it might be a good thing. Maybe we said nothing; maybe I touched her hand and she let me. Maybe she held it for a moment too long. I don't know. Miranda quit academia and vanished into air like Prospero's Ariel without saying a word to anyone, or maybe just not to me. I never saw her again.

For years, I used to hear my name whispered on the wind, and when I looked no one was there, no matter how quickly I turned. I was sure it was her voice finding me, like spooky action at a distance. Turns out I was just bipolar. A storm never washed me ashore on her island, but I can still feel her bending me to her will; I think it is her will.

The Quitter is Illuminated

"Some quitters are born with style—every quit these lucky quitters accomplish is illuminated."

—Evan Harris, *The Quit*

I.

A loud fart refracts around the room, so loud that if I didn't know exactly where it was coming from, it would have been difficult to triangulate its origin. This happens so often my students don't even snicker anymore. No one looks up. They keep writing as if it were some kind of foreign cultural practice we have come to accept as normal. We are lucky it is only one. Sometimes it's a whole assonant string, a one-hundred-foot-long deep-sea siphonophore rumbling along the ocean floor. There is no pedagogy workshop or graduate-level class you can take to address this particular problem. I know because I've looked. It comes from the same spot, the same desk, the same student, who, of course, never misses a day of class. "Dolores, would you like to work in the hallway?" This has been my only successful gambit. I have a desk permanently reserved in the hallway for her, for Dolores of the Sorrows. She likes to complain the other students distract her and that she can't concentrate, which, of course, is the darkest kind of irony since she's been holding us hostage with her distractions all semester. *Bel*

Canto it isn't. Ten years of teaching, ten years of never having a serious problem with behavior, ten years of coming up with creative solutions to help students from less-than-supportive socio-economic backgrounds, students who live in crime-infested parts of the city, students who have children and work several jobs, international students who have escaped some horrible atrocity, and Dolores counters all my moves with ease, with a prodigious ability worthy of Gary Kasparov or his digital nemesis, Deep Blue. I've sacrificed all my most powerful pieces and she has gobbled them up, one by one. Checkmate is imminent. In fact, had this been actual chess, I would have long since extended my hand to concede the match. But as it is, I will have to play until there is no escape, or the clock runs out.

II.

Dolores, Our Lady of the Sorrows—the name says it all, as they so often have in my life.

When I first started teaching at this college, I had an amazing Congolese student named Lovemore, which I would come to find out was pronounced, Love-a-more. Actually, his name was Lovemore Dick. Lovemore Dick! Right there in black and white. When I looked at my list of names on the first day of class, I thought my colleagues were having some fun with me. It was a pretty lame joke, but at least they were aware of my existence, which was novel. (Adjuncts, for the most part, are ignored, though we teach the majority of the students at the postsecondary level. Seventy-five percent of all classes are taught by a giant and largely invisible class of part-time labor, so I thought any place where full-timers would take the time to perpetrate such a ruse, even such a bad one, was probably a good place to be.) As I was about to skip over the name, however, some part of me wondered if it were possible for there to be an individual with such an unfortunate name. My curiosity got the better of me, and since there's nothing a student hates more on the first day than to be the one the teacher skips over, I decided to call it out anyway. My solution was simple; I called only the first name. When no one responded, I knew for certain that it was a joke.

It should be pretty easy to discover the culprit, I thought. The first faculty member to ask how my class went would be the traitor—the old *Godfather* routine. Rule number one is never be the one to set up the meeting. They'll have to get up much earlier in the morning to fool me, or so I told myself. However, since I had to rush to catch a train to another college in time for my next class, I didn't get the opportunity to discover the identity of my would-be tormentor.

When the class met again, I skipped over the name, completely certain this student did not exist. After I finished attendance, however, a hand shot up, and, of course, it was Lovemore Dick. He was real. I couldn't believe it. He sat in the front row and raised his hand often, but not so much that it became annoying. His writing was not good, but he never got discouraged no matter what the grade; he was always willing to put in a serious effort. And he had a radiant smile, which was so refreshing in comparison to the dull grimaces of American students.

III.

Around midterm, Lovemore came to visit me in my office. He looked so grim and serious I was afraid he was coming to tell me he was dropping my class.

I have lost many great students because their out-of-class lives get in the way of their studies, something the people who are supposed to be measuring "success" can't seem to take into account, even though they should know better. I realized years ago that my students cling to the fiction that I am all-seeing and all-knowing. They take it on faith that I spend every waking moment thinking about them, and the disappointment is profound when it becomes clear that I am not. If I forget a handout I promised, if I blank on a name, if I can't remember off the top of my head every comment I made on a paper, the illusion melts and they have to go back to a reality where no one is thinking about them very much at all.

I missed much of what Lovemore was saying but I tuned back in time to hear, "I have PTSD. I wanted you to know because I love your class and I don't want you to think less of me." I didn't know what to say next. I sensed he wanted to tell me more, but I didn't know how to give him permission. "Were you a soldier?" Many of my students are current or former military. "No, but when I was living in Africa, a bunch of soldiers broke into our house and butchered my family." I didn't know what to say so I sat there with my mouth open playing see no evil, hear no evil, speak no evil. "I was hiding in the bathroom and they didn't see me." He went on to describe how he watched them murder his mother, father, siblings, and grandparents. When night came, he had to step over their bodies in order to get away. Eventually, he said, he made it to Virunga where many other refugees had been living.

If only this type of story was rare—but I've known many students, foreign and domestic, who have had similarly gruesome experiences. These stories make me wonder if anything I am supposed to teach them could ever make up for such horror.

IV.

The hard truth is he barely passed my class. I didn't know what kind of opportunities there would be for him. He was already a cab driver, a doorman, and who knows what else, all while going to school full time. The deck wasn't stacked against him—he had no cards whatsoever. It took this much effort just to get a seat at the card table, and the other players were strapped and quick on the draw.

But a year later he was back with me in my college-level composition course. (This doesn't mean I am a good instructor, by the way. Many students will keep taking the same teacher whether they like them or not. It's the old, devil you know routine.) I, of course, was very happy to have him back. There was one problem, though—his papers were suddenly really, really good. I admit I thought he might be cheating. I wanted to believe those were his papers. If the world owed one person, it was him. But I didn't know if that much improvement was possible in such a short time. I am not that good a teacher, and there was only one course between the basic-level class he took with me and this one. But since there was no real way to be sure, I wasn't going to run the risk of alienating him forever by accusing him, so I graded the papers all semester as if he had written them.

The real test would come when my students did the in-class essays at the end of the semester. There was no way to fake the in-class essay, no way to have someone else write it for you, no way to purchase one online—no easy way, anyway. When I got to his paper, I was literally sweating. I kept picking it up and putting it back down. I considered accidentally losing the folder. If the quality of the work was not in keeping with the other essays, I would have to accuse one of my favorite students of all time of cheating. I think I would have rather quit my job. In fact, I considered that option. I thought about walking away from teaching forever just so I wouldn't have to be responsible for Lovemore's fate anymore. I didn't want to be guarding the gates. Who was I to be guarding the gates? Who was I guarding the gates for? When I finally forced myself to read his essay, I nearly wept. It was so good. Not only was he not cheating, he had grown, truly grown, as a writer. It was real. The miracle of Lovemore remained untarnished, unsullied, and unwavering.

V.

"Dolores, would you like to go into the hall?" She says no.

Dolores is schizophrenic. She can't help that she's been terrorizing the class. My students, to their everlasting credit, have been patient, but rifts are starting to appear and I know it won't take much to bring it all crashing down, and when the Nothing sweeps in, the darkness will be complete.

Community colleges have open enrollment, which I truly believe in, but many of these institutions lack the proper services to support a student like Dolores. It was made clear to me that I would be on my own with her. At least she was mostly quiet when we were writing. Last week during a discussion, Dolores kept interrupting—and, of course, her comments were very rarely on topic. We were pretty accustomed to this too, but she seemed more agitated than normal this day, and one of my other students—an older woman named Barbara who was returning to school for the first time in a decade—must have been having a bad day too, because she uncharacteristically confronted Dolores. (Confronting Dolores is like waging a flame war with an internet troll. It's a losing battle because they have nothing at stake.) Dolores, of course, lashed back. It looked like things were going to unravel, but I managed to intervene and quiet them down.

The blow-up seemed to purge Dolores's desire to interrupt that day, but there has been lasting tension between those two since. A burp from Dolores this time. Any noise or movement that comes from that side of the class makes me so tense my shoulders are starting to pinch inwards towards my sternum, like a horseshoe, but without the luck. My teeth are in rough shape, but I can't afford to do anything about it. Like the wilderness, America is no place to be without your teeth; I'd soon be helpless.

VI.

Dolores's hand goes up. As usual, she does not wait for me to call on her. "What are we doing?" Twenty-five minutes have gone by and now she asks what we're doing. I don't know what keeps my voice steady because this isn't the first time she's done this either.

Look into the teacher's eyes. This is where you will see the quit if it is going to happen. The class is over in a couple of minutes, so I tell her I will explain it to her afterwards. I admit I add the word "again" at the end of my sentence. I can't help it. I don't have a lot of time between classes, but it's better than trying to deal with her while class is still in session.

When class ends, Barbara—Dolores's rival—comes to my desk to ask a question about her paper. Out of nowhere, Dolores hip checks her and sends her crashing into the first row of desks. Barbara goes clattering to a knee, which makes a terrible crunching noise when it hits the floor. For a moment, no one seems to know what to do, but Barbara recovers before I do, and she is up like she knows how to handle herself in a fight. And I have no doubt she does. Barbara is someone you would describe as no-nonsense. Some part of me wants to watch her pummel Dolores into a paste for the trauma she has caused me, but I don't want to be responsible for a fight. I could lose my job. Without being conscious of it, I somehow manage to wedge myself between them as they scream into each other's faces. I don't hear words; I feel fists clench, pupils fully dilate, adrenalin pump in veins, and muscles ready to twitch. Thankfully no one throws a punch, which is lucky for me because they would have hit me right in the face. I recover enough of my faculties to send Dolores away.

Barbara and I go to see the Dean of Student Services, who seems very supportive, and for a moment I am sure she is going to remove Dolores from my class, but ultimately she does not. If an outright assault isn't enough to constitute removal, what on earth is? This is the main reason I decided not to teach high school. I didn't want to be at the mercy of students who didn't want to be in the classroom and who were a danger to others. I ask Barbara to sit as far as possible from Dolores and I apologize, like it is my fault that nothing is done.

VII.

The semester manages, against all expectations, to finally come to an end.

Adult time, unlike childhood time, is long in minutes and short in years. Hours last for years, but years go by in seconds. On the last day of class, I hand back portfolios and give my students tentative final grades. I have been dreading my confrontation with Dolores all morning but since it is the last day, I am also feeling something akin to hope, like hope with opposite particle spin. When Dolores comes in and gets the bad news, she leaves without incident or complaint, and I take my first full-body breath since the day I met her in September. It's over. It's really over. There is snow on the ground and Chicago looks Midwestern for a moment in that predictably pastoral way which is both true and beside the point. And as I sit at my desk, I think once more of Lovemore.

He had lived in Virunga National Park for years after the tragedy with his family and managed to survive the fighting in Congo. I was remembering the amazing story he told the class the day we discussed a short essay by Jane Goodall. Normally I would have doubted the veracity of such a story, but he was a person without guile, so I didn't have any good reason not to believe him. I wanted to believe it.

The essay describes Goodall's attempts to get close to the chimps in Gombe, and Lovemore said that he had experienced the same thing with chimps in Virunga. I kind of laughed it off at first but he explained that over a long period of time, he inched closer and closer, like Goodall did—allowing the chimps to get accustomed to having him in their territory—until they basically accepted him as one of the troop. The chimps would come and spy on him and sometimes steal things he left unguarded. Anything with a bright color would be gone. They were very curious, he said, and loved causing mischief. One young chimp in particular would throw anything he could get his hands on at Lovemore, and then he'd laugh if he managed to hit him. He dubbed the chimp Bullseye. Apparently, Bullseye's aim was pretty good too. Eventually they became comfortable enough to build nests near Lovemore's camp where they would sometimes nap during the day. Chimps build nests in trees like birds.

One morning, however, Lovemore said he woke to the sound of screaming. He was afraid some poachers or some other predator like a crocodile was attacking the chimps, but it turned out one of the mothers had just given birth. He described how the entire troop seemed to be celebrating the new baby. Chimps were jumping and pulling cartwheels, playing chase. Some of the other female chimps were attempting to caress the new baby, but the young mother was having none of it. Lovemore depended on this story; it gave his time in the forest the shape of reason.

VIII.

By the time I return to my office, there is already a phone message waiting for me. I have been summoned to the office of the same Dean, the one who listened with so much sympathy and then refused to help me. Dolores has already been in to complain about failing the class.

I had anticipated this, so I'd kept a file of all our email exchanges to demonstrate all the work I had put in to try and help her achieve a passing grade. I had photocopies of all her papers to show that they were not passing, that they never had been close to passing. I brought in her portfolio, which in our department is also graded by two other faculty members, and showed that they too had failed her. The Dean looked at my evidence and said Dolores was going to claim the other students were constantly distracting her and that I didn't do anything about it. When I reminded her that she had been the one to assault a student, the dean neither denied it nor corroborated it. She said it was up to me. If I gave her a C, she would go away. She added that Dolores had a record of complaints and would most likely make my life difficult. And then I was dismissed.

IX.

Of course, I didn't tell Lovemore the rest of Goodall's story. I didn't mention the day she watched Passion and Pom, a mother-daughter team, eat the child of a lesser female and then embrace the half-dead mother as if to say it was just business. And I didn't mention that it wasn't, as she hoped, an aberration; she watched from her spot in a baobab tree as they did it again and again. Dominant females protect their positions in the hierarchy just like male chimps do, with immediate and often violent results.

I want to say I failed Dolores. I want to say Dolores forgave my failure. I want to say Lovemore saved the day. I want to say I survived in Virunga among the chimps. I want to say I quit right there and stormed off in righteous anger. I want to say I was illuminated.

Acknowledgments

Essays in the "Dead Man's Chest" section were published in *Another Chicago Magazine* and *More Than Sports Talk*. "The Bull's Eye" was first published in *Atticus Review*. "Smells Like Teen Spirit" and "The Quitters" appeared in *Queen Mob's Teahouse*. "Portuguese Paradise" was first published in *The Gravity of the Thing*. "The Quitter is Illuminated" was published in the *Bad Jobs and Bullshit* anthology. Portions of this manuscript also appeared in my chapbooks, "Most Human Human Contest" (Slash Pine Press) and "skate/glove" (Finishing Line Press).

Special thanks to the Sundress Academy for the Arts and La Romita for the funding and the uninterrupted time to work.

About the Author

Carlo Matos has published ten books, including *It's Best Not to Interrupt Her Experiments* (Negative Capability Press) and *The Secret Correspondence of Loon & Fiasco* (Mayapple Press). He also co-edited an anthology with Luis Gonçalves titled *Writers of the Portuguese Diaspora in the United States and Canada*. His poems, stories, and essays have appeared in such journals as *Iowa Review*, *Boston Review*, *Another Chicago Magazine*, *Rhino*, *Diagram*, and *Handsome*, among many others. Carlo has received grants from the Illinois Arts Council, the Fundação Luso-Americana, the Sundress Academy for the Arts, and La Romita (Italy)—and is a winner of the Heartland Poetry Prize. He currently lives in Chicago, IL, is a professor at the City Colleges of Chicago, a teaching artist at The Poetry Barn, and a former MMA fighter and kickboxer. These days he can be found writing poems on demand with Poems While You Wait and training in the exquisite art of the Italian rapier. Follow him on twitter @CarloMatos46. He blogs at carlomatos.blogspot.com

CPSIA information can be obtained
at www.ICGtesting.com
Printed in the USA
BVOW03s0830221117
501062BV00001B/7/P